MENINGITIS

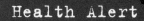

MENINGITIS

Lorrie Klosterman

Marshall Cavendish
Benchmark
New York

With thanks to Dave Spilker, President, and Dr. Kyle Hendrix, Board Member, Meningitis Foundation of America, for their expert review of the manuscript.

Marshall Cavendish Benchmark
99 White Plains Road
Tarrytown, New York 10591-9001
www.marshallcavendish.us

Library of Congress Cataloging-in-Publication Data

Klosterman, Lorrie.
  Meningitis / by Lorrie Klosterman.
     p. cm. -- (Health alert)
  Summary: "Explores the history, causes, symptoms, treatments, and future
of different types of meningitis"--Provided by publisher.
  Includes index.
  ISBN-13: 978-0-7614-2211-2
  ISBN-10: 0-7614-2211-0
 1. Meningitis--Juvenile literature. I. Title. II. Series: Health alert
(New York, N.Y.)

  RC376.K56 2007
  616.8'2--dc22

                              2006015819

Front cover: An X ray of a skull
Title page: The *Haemophilus influenzae* meningitis bacteria
Contents page: *Neisseria meningitis* bacteria
Photo Research by Candlepants Incorporated

Cover Photo: Bill Longcore/Photo Researchers Inc.

The photographs in this book are used by permission and through the courtesy of; *Photo Researchers Inc.:* Dr. Tony Brain, 3, 24; Bill Dowsett, 5; Mehua Kulyk, 10, 48; David M. Phillips, 11; Jim Dowdalls, 12; S. Fraser, 15; Biophoto Associates, 16; Noah Poritz, 17; John Radcliffe Hospital, 20; Barry Dowsett, 22; Andy Crump, TDR, WHO, 25: James Prince, 27; Sotirius Zafeirus, 30; Dr. P. Marazzi, 33; CC Studio, 34; Science Photo Library, 38; St. Mary's Hospital Medical School, 39; Antonia Reeve, 41; VEM, 43; SimonFraser/ Royal Victoria Infirmary, Newcastle, 44, 46; Val De Grace-Voisin, 47; Phanie, 49; Richard T. Noowitz, 51; Will & Demi McIntyre, 52, 54, 55. *Corbis:<I>* Stuart Westmoreland, 29.

Printed in China

6 5 4 3 2 1

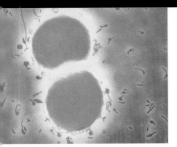

CONTENTS

1

WHAT IS IT LIKE TO HAVE MENINGITIS?

It had been a great day at school for Shawna. She had worked hard and done well on her history presentation. But now, as she rode home on the school bus, she felt very tired, and she was getting a bad headache, too. She wondered whether she had stayed up too late preparing her presentation.

At home, Shawna skipped her usual after-school snack because her stomach felt a little upset. She went outside in the yard to play with her dog, but she had no energy to throw the ball. Her dad suggested taking a nap, and he was surprised when Shawna headed upstairs to do just that. She was usually a bundle of energy and never took naps.

A few hours later, a terrible headache awakened Shawna from a deep sleep. When she tried to sit up, her neck hurt so much, she was not able to turn her head toward the door to call for her parents. When they did come up, they saw right away that something was very wrong. Shawna could not move without crying in pain, and she seemed confused. Her mother took her temperature: It was 99.1 degrees Fahrenheit, which was not very high.

Then Shawna's mother noticed a rash on her daughter's legs. Her heart raced as she remembered a newspaper report she had read about a local high school student who had died of meningitis a few months earlier. The paper had said to be on the lookout for an illness that may seem like the flu at first. But people with meningitis suffer from a very bad headache, a stiff neck, and often a rash—just like the one Shawna had now.

Shawna's parents did not take any chances. They rushed her to the hospital immediately. They knew that the **bacteria,** or germs, that cause some kinds of meningitis can spread through the brain and elsewhere in the body. This could injure tissues and organs beyond repair within hours.

At the emergency room, a doctor examined Shawna right away. Her temperature had climbed to 102 degrees, and her heart was racing. She was crying because of the headache. Her legs ached, too. Soon she started to have trouble breathing and could barely move.

A doctor had Shawna curl up on her side, with bent knees, so he could take a fluid sample from the space between the bones in her spinal column. During this **spinal tap,** the doctor carefully drew a tiny amount of fluid from Shawna's **spinal cord** into a hollow needle. The doctor saw that the fluid was cloudy, which was not a good sign. Laboratory technicians examined the fluid right away. It contained bacteria. Shawna had **bacterial meningitis.**

The doctors and nurses immediately gave Shawna a large dose of **antibiotics** to try to kill the bacteria. They placed her on a respirator machine to help her breathe. A nurse prepared an **intravenous** line, which is a tube attached to a needle. She put this IV into Shawna's arm to get the medication flowing into her body as fast as possible.

Over the next few days, Shawna slipped into a **coma.** While their daughter was unconscious, Shawna's parents could only wait. Doctors and nurses observed Shawna around the clock. Anyone who visited her had to wear gowns and masks as protection from getting infected, also. Her family took antibiotics as a precaution to be sure they did not become sick, too. The hospital informed Shawna's school about the illness and advised that any students or teachers who had spent time with Shawna should take antibiotics.

Four days after she entered the hospital, Shawna woke up from her coma. She was very tired and confused. She did not remember everything that had happened since her arrival at the hospital. When a doctor asked her to move different parts of her body, she was unable to move her right arm or hand, and she had trouble moving her right leg. Also, she did not recognize her older brother or know how old she was or remember what her class presentation had been about just a few days earlier. That told doctors that part of her brain had been injured. She had also lost some of her hearing.

Shawna still needed the respirator to breathe. The doctors continued to give her antibiotics to kill the bacteria and intravenous fluids to feed her because she could not eat normally right away. The good news was that the rash was fading, showing that antibiotics were killing the bacteria in her legs. Her fever was lower, too. She was going to survive.

Shawna stayed in the hospital another week, getting better as the time passed. She began to breathe well on her own and started to eat solid food again. While in the hospital, a physical therapist helped Shawna begin the exercises she would need to practice to walk properly and use her right arm again. After several months of doing these excercises, Shawna was able to move normally. Her hearing, however, did not improve. Although she could hear some things fine, she wanted hearing aids to be sure she was not missing anything.

One more thing Shawna did after recovering from bacterial meningitis was to tell her story to others. She wrote about it in the school newspaper and sent the story to other schools. She also got her health class to make posters reminding people that **vaccination** against meningitis saves lives.

Shawna did all this because it was her parents' knowledge and fast action that helped save her life. She had not realized until she got sick that bacterial meningitis was so dangerous. Now she wanted other people to know, too.

2

WHAT IS MENINGITIS?

Meningitis is a serious **infection** of the **meninges,** a protective covering that surrounds the brain and spinal cord. This infection strikes about 13,000 Americans every year. Approximately three-quarters of meningitis victims are babies, children, teenagers, and young adults. Most people recover completely from meningitis.

Some forms of the infection are deadly, however. One in ten people who becomes infected with one of these forms will die. Of the survivors, two in ten people wind up with serious problems such as deafness, brain damage, the loss of arms and legs, and electrical disturbances in

The backbone, or vertebral column, is made up of 33 bones that descend from the brain down the spine. These bones support the body and protect the spinal cord.

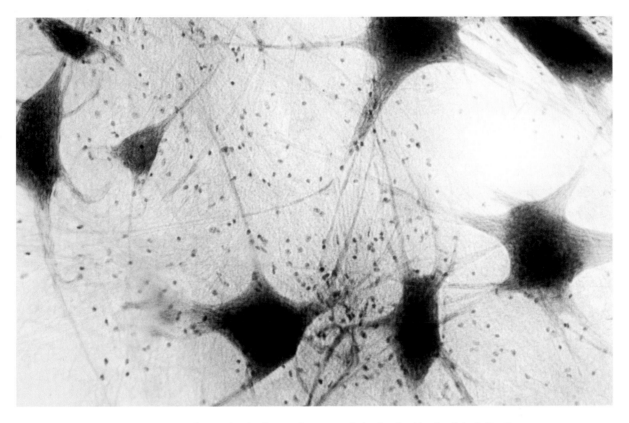

Neurons carry messages from the brain to the rest of the body. Meningitis infection damages these neurons, and messages cannot get through.

the brain, called **seizures,** that affect muscle control.

All of these problems may happen because meningitis attacks the most important parts of the human body: the brain and the spinal cord. These are the body's control centers. They are made up of nerve **cells** called **neurons,** which send electrical and chemical messages to millions of other neurons in all parts of the body. Together, all these neurons form a network that enables the body to work. Anything that goes wrong along the network can shut down some of the body's functions.

THE MENINGES

Fortunately, your brain and spinal cord have several levels of protection. The outer level is made up of bones, including the skull and the vertebral column. This column of bones protects your spinal cord, where so many neurons travel to make every part of your body work.

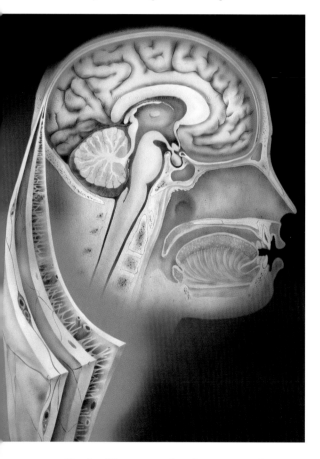

Meningitis causes the three protective layers of the meninges to swell and injure the brain cells.

The meninges, which are bathed in **cerebrospinal** fluid, provide the second protective level. These thin sheets of living tissue are made up of three layers called the dura, arachnoid, and pia. The three layers cover the surface of your brain, as well as your spinal cord. The meninges are something like layers of living plastic wrap because they are thin and transparent. But the meninges are crisscrossed with blood vessels. These vessels supply the nearby neurons of the brain and spinal cord with everything they need to stay alive, including oxygen and nutrients. The meninges form a barrier, too, keeping out harmful invaders such as drugs, bacteria, and **viruses.** Damage to the meninges lets in invaders and threatens everything your brain controls.

INFLAMMATION

When an area of the body is injured, it becomes swollen or inflamed. Many injuries can cause **inflammation:** bruises, scrapes, cuts, burns, or insect and animal bites. Even a splinter can cause minor inflammation. Harmful viruses, bacteria, parasites, and other foreign organisms can trigger more serious inflammation.

Whatever the cause of inflammation, extra blood flows through the injured area to heal damaged cells, causing the swelling. However, in areas where space is tight, such as in the brain or spine, too much swelling can damage or kill cells that were not injured in the first place. When brain cells get squeezed between the skull and inflamed meninges, damage to neurons may result. During meningitis, this squeezing of brain tissues causes severe headache and neck pain. Brain damage may make it impossible for neurons in the brain to send messages throughout the body to perform many important functions.

So how do harmful invaders get past bones and cerebrospinal fluid and into the meninges? The two main microorganisms that cause meningitis—viruses and bacteria— can enter the body through cuts, wounds, burns, bites, injuries, inhaled air, or through the mouth. The microorganisms can then travel in the bloodstream and attack the meninges. When that happens, someone may come down with meningitis.

There is no way to avoid bacteria and viruses completely. You can pick them up from animals, insects, other people, and surfaces that you touch. Millions of bacteria live harmlessly on our skin and inside our mouths, noses, and other body openings. In fact, some bacteria living inside our bodies produce substances that keep us healthy. Meningitis experts know that many people carry around meningitis viruses and bacteria in their throats and never come down with the infection. They do not yet know all the reasons why some seemingly healthy people get the infection and others do not.

Uncommon Causes of Meningitis

- an allergic reaction to certain medications
- tuberculosis, an infection of the lungs
- some types of cancer
- *Salmonella* bacteria picked up after handling snakes, turtles, and iguanas
- organisms called protozoa that swimmers may pick up while swimming in fresh water
- a type of fungus someone gets from touching or breathing in particles found in bird droppings

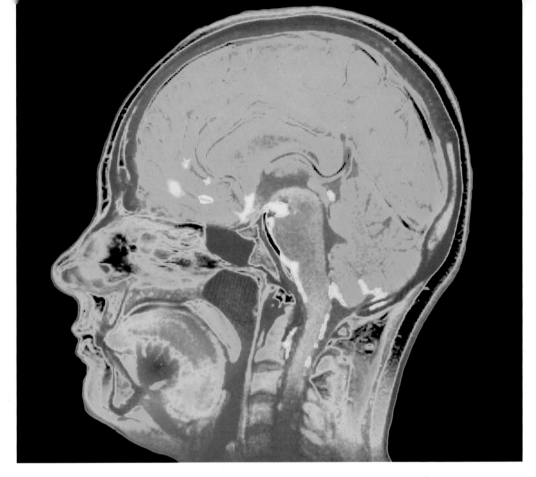

The yellow section of this MRI image shows meningitis bacteria infecting surfaces of the brain and spinal cord.

VIRAL MENINGITIS

Viral meningitis is the most common type of meningitis. It is caused by viruses and is much less harmful than the bacterial type. Adults, followed by preteens and teenagers, are more likely to get viral meningitis than the bacterial type. Although a person may suffer from headache, neck pain, and sensitivity to light, he or she almost always recovers completely from viral meningitis without being hospitalized.

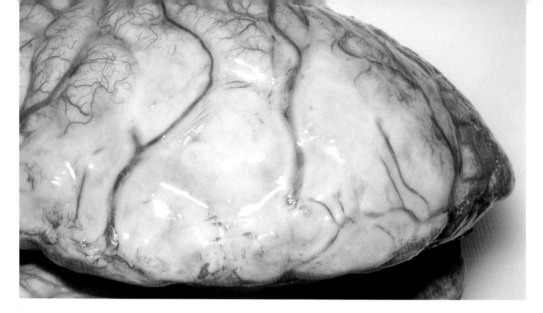

The inflammation on this brain, shown in red, caused a fatal case of meningitis. If families agree, doctors may perform surgery on the body, called an autopsy, to learn more about the meningitis bacteria that killed the patient.

Several types of viruses can infect the meninges. Some cause other illnesses such as chicken pox, measles, mumps, and polio. In the United States and in many other countries, children are vaccinated with shots that protect them against these diseases. These vaccinations offer some protection against viral meningitis.

Some viruses live in **feces,** the waste matter that people produce in their intestines after they digest food. These viruses can spread when an infected person does not wash his or her hands after using the toilet or after changing a baby's diaper. The harmful viruses from the infected person's intestines may get onto surfaces that another person touches. If this other person then touches his or her mouth with contaminated hands, he or she may pick up one of the kinds of viruses that causes viral meningitis. Hand washing after using the toilet or changing a diaper and before eating can prevent many different viruses from spreading in this way. Keeping hands away from the eyes, nose, and mouth also keeps viruses, as well as bacteria, from spreading.

Viruses that cause meningitis are present in the saliva and **mucus** of someone who is infected. The virus may be transmitted to another person through sneezing, coughing, kissing, or by sharing drinking containers and eating utensils.

Mosquitoes carrying viruses can cause meningitis when they bite someone, although this is less common than getting sick through human contact. A few other kinds of viruses infect the meninges when they get inside neurons near the surfaces of the body. The viruses then travel wherever the neurons reach, including the spinal cord and brain.

Viruses damage the meninges

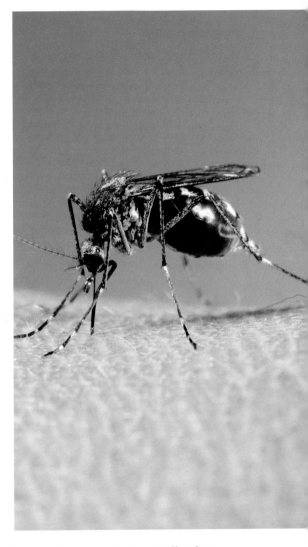

Mosquitoes carry the West Nile virus, which can infect the meninges and cause viral meningitis.

when they invade the meninges' cells and copy themselves. As more viruses are made, they fill the cells, which can no longer function well. A cell can get so filled with viruses that it bursts open. That kills the cell and releases more viruses. These viruses spread to other cells, where they repeat the cycle of reproducing and damaging cells. All these processes trigger inflammation, harming neurons in the brain and spinal cord. Usually, the inflammation does not cause the kind of harmful swelling seen in bacterial meningitis.

Fortunately, almost everyone who gets viral meningitis gets better in a few weeks, even without medication. This recovery happens because the infected person's **immune system** destroys the viruses. Viral meningitis is rarely deadly.

BACTERIAL MENINGITIS

Bacterial meningitis can be deadly. Bacteria often reproduce more rapidly than viruses. These bacteria produce poisons called **toxins** that are harmful to the body and can cause a lot of damage in a short time. Some people who come down with bacterial meningitis die within hours of getting their first symptoms such as a severe headache, a fever, a stiff neck, mental confusion, and a rash. In those cases, victims die before health professionals have time to figure out what is wrong. That is why it is important for everyone to know the signs of meningitis, especially since some symptoms are similar to those of the flu.

Not all symptoms may appear in the early stages of meningitis. But someone with several of them, especially the painfully stiff neck and rash, should get to a hospital immediately.

Ten to fifteen percent of people who get bacterial meningitis in the United States die from it. In countries where many people live far from hospitals or doctors with effective medications, the death rate from bacterial meningitis is much higher. Around the globe, about 120,000 to 200,000 people die of this illness each year.

Most people who get bacterial meningitis do not die. But about 10 to 15 percent of survivors do end

Flu or Bacterial Meningitis?

· ·

POSSIBLE FLU SYMPTOMS:

- fever that may get high
- mild to moderate headache
- overall muscle aches
- cough
- tiredness
- symptoms level off, then usually improve

POSSIBLE MENINGITIS SYMPTOMS:

- severe headache, described by many patients as the worst they have ever had
- extreme neck pain that makes it difficult for someone to touch his or her chin to the chest
- variable fever that can be low or high
- cold hands and feet during the fever
- extreme sensitivity to light
- very sore legs and arms
- skin rash that gets worse quickly
- drowsiness and mental confusion
- sudden tightening of muscles called seizures
- in babies: some of the above symptoms, along with limpness, moaning, blank staring, or an arched back

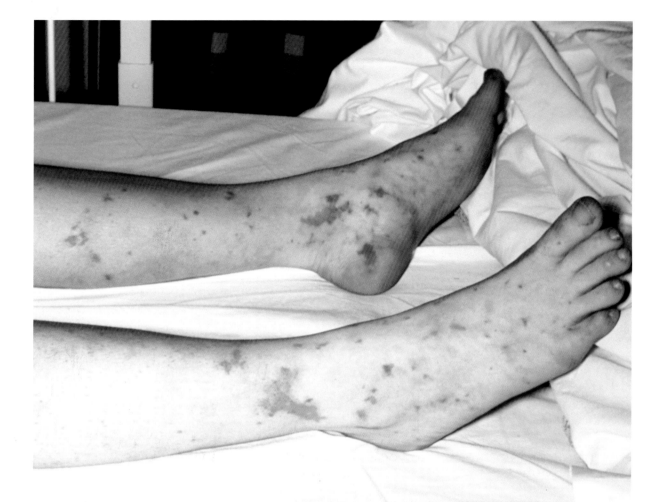

Some types of bacterial meningitis occur with blood poisoning that damages blood vessels and causes blood to leak into the skin. This forms a rash that worsens quickly.

up with permanent damage to their brains, nervous systems, kidneys, or limbs. Long-term effects can include seizures, hearing loss due to damage of the delicate structures inside the ears, learning disabilities, and even blindness.

Blood Poisoning

One form of meningitis can take a deadly turn. Half the people who get meningococcal meningitis also develop a life-threatening condition called **septicemia,** or blood poisoning. Of those people who get meningitis-related septicemia, nearly half will die from it.

Blood poisoning does its damage when the meningococcal bacteria multiply uncontrollably in the body and produce toxins. As these poisons race through the bloodstream, they damage blood vessel walls along the way. The purple rash and bruises that appear during septicemia are a sign that blood is leaking through the blood vessels. When that happens, several life-threatening problems occur.

First, **blood pressure** drops as blood leaks into tissues instead of going to major organs. As a result, the kidneys, lungs, brain, and heart do not get enough blood to function properly and may begin to fail. The heart races to deliver blood, while vessels in the arms and leg narrow so that more blood will go to vital organs. That is why a person with blood poisoning may have cold hands and feet, even during a fever.

At the same time, damaged blood vessels and poor circulation may cause the severe destruction of skin and muscle tissues called **gangrene.** If gangrene develops, **amputation** of arms, legs, fingers, or toes may be necessary. Surgically removing these damaged tissues helps prevent the infection from spreading further.

Several diseases and infections, as well as meningitis, can cause blood poisoning. No matter what the cause, septicemia is always a medical emergency. Immediate treatment with antibiotics in a hospital can save lives.

Types of Bacterial Meningitis

Several kinds of bacteria can cause meningitis. All of them can be damaging or deadly if not treated right away. Most of them belong to four groups.

Meningococcal meningitis

The group that causes meningitis **epidemics** has the Latin name *Neisseria meningitis.* Someone with that kind of bacteria is said to have meningococcal meningitis, the most common type of meningitis in people from ages three to eighteen. These bacteria can quickly spread among people who spend a lot of time together—children, young people at camps, in school, college, and the military. Each year in the United States about 300 people die from meningococcal meningitis, and vaccines do not work against one

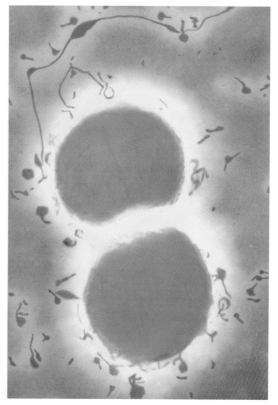

Neisseria meningitis bacteria are usually seen in pairs as in this micrograph. Fortunately, a vaccine has been developed against these bacteria.

of the three forms of this infection. Because blood poisoning also appears quite often with meningococcal meningitis, survivors can wind up with permanent injuries.

Pneumococcal meningitis

Another group of bacteria that causes bacterial meningitis is *Streptococcus pneumoniae*. It is usually called pneumococcal meningitis and is the most common type of meningitis overall. The bacteria in this type are also the most common cause of ear infections in children. The bacteria can also cause pneumonia, which is a serious lung infection. Risk factors for pneumococcal meningitis include: head injury, diabetes, and some diseases that have weakened the immune system. People who wear implanted hearing aids have a higher risk of getting this form of meningitis. So do people who have had their **spleens** removed since this organ helps filter out bacteria and viruses. For unknown reasons, children of certain racial or ethnic groups get pneumococcal meningitis more often than other children. These groups include Alaska Natives, Native Americans, and African Americans. About one out of every twenty children under five years old who gets pneumococcal meningitis does not survive. Fortunately, two recommended vaccines for the elderly and children under two, have greatly cut the number of pneumococcal meningitis cases in countries with widespread vaccination programs.

Hib meningitis

A third group of bacteria that causes meningitis goes by the Latin name *Haemophilus influenzae* type b, or Hib for short.

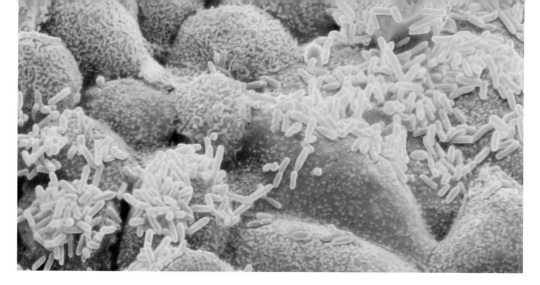

The *Haemophilus influenzae* bacteria, shown in yellow in this electron micrograph, has infected the nasal lining, shown in pink. Different forms can cause bronchitis, pneumonia, or meningitis, mainly in children.

These bacteria used to be the leading cause of meningitis among infants and young children in the United States until an effective vaccine was developed against them in 1990. Since then, infants and toddlers have this vaccination. It is now rare for a child to get this type of meningitis. *Haemophilus influenzae* type b can cause other serious infections such as **epiglottitis.** This is a very serious infection at the back of the throat. Inflammation from meningitis can cause the throat to swell up so much that it prevents breathing. Before the Hib vaccine, epiglottitis killed many children each year, and it still does in countries where vaccinations are uncommon.

Group B *Streptococci*
The most common cause of bacterial meningitis in babies up to three months of age is Group B Streptococci, or GBS for short. GBS can also cause other serious infections in newborns,

such as pneumonia. This type of bacteria is carried by the mother and passed to the infant during birth. It is estimated that up to 30 percent of women carry this type of bacteria. Risk factors in the mother may lead to GBS infection in babies. These include certain fevers during pregnancy, prolonged labor, multiple births like twins, or having a previous baby born with GBS. The chance of a baby contracting GBS can be decreased by screening mothers during pregnancy. If the mother is positive for GBS or has any of the risk factors listed above, the mother can be given antibiotics during labor to decrease the chance that the bacteria will spread to the baby.

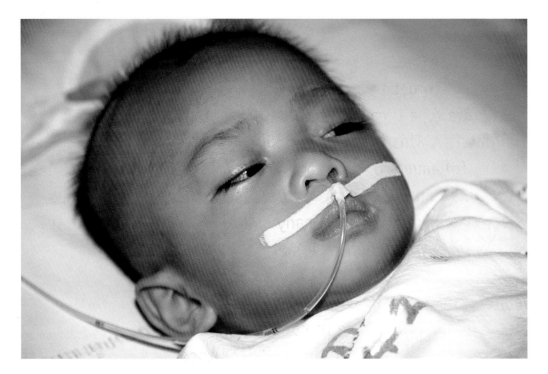

This baby has bacterial meningitis and needs to be hospitalized to help fight infection.

WHO WILL GET MENINGITIS?

Although many people come into contact with viruses and bacteria that cause meningitis, only some people get it. These germs seem to be harmless much of the time, but they occasionally enter the bloodstream. From there, they can be carried to the meninges and elsewhere in the body. When that happens, the bacteria can cause infections if the immune system does not get rid of them fast enough.

What is it that allows some people with the meningitis bacteria to remain healthy, while others become sick? Researchers are trying to understand that. One theory is that the bacteria in some people **mutate,** or change, in such a way that the immune system can no longer destroy them easily. Another

Encephalitis and Myelitis

Two other illnesses are similar to meningitis. **Encephalitis** is an inflammation of the brain itself (*enceph-* refers to the brain, *-itis* means inflammation). **Myelitis** is inflammation of the spinal cord. These are both very serious illnesses because neurons in the brain and spinal cord can be injured and killed. As in meningitis, bacteria or viruses work their way into the brain and spinal cord. Symptoms are very similar to those of meningitis. Doctors can treat encephalitis and myelitis bacteria with antibiotics.

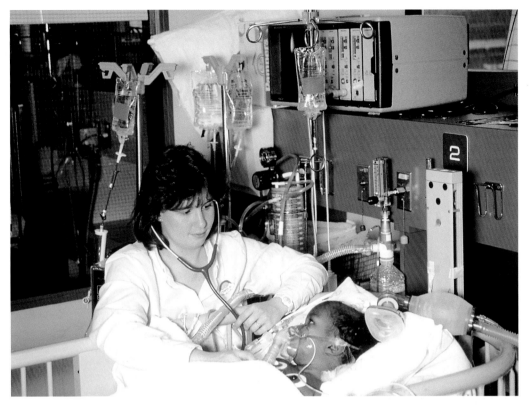

Patients with bacterial meningitis are usually cared for in intensive care units where the medical staff can give them constant attention.

possibility is that when certain bacteria do mutate, they may become more effective at getting into the bloodstream and meninges.

Some experts believe that certain people have better immune systems than others and are better able to fight off infections. That seems true for meningitis. Infants and very young children, whose immune systems are still developing, are most in danger of getting meningitis. So are the elderly, because as people get much older, their ability to fight off infections decreases. Some people have illnesses that make their immune systems less able to fight off infections, and they get meningitis more often. AIDS (acquired immunodeficiency syndrome) is one such illness. People who take medications for some other illness are more likely to get meningitis if those medications damage their immune systems. One example is the strong cell-killing medications used to treat cancer. Then there are those people who, very rarely, are born without some of the immune cells they need, and are much more likely to get all kinds of infections.

Doctors have figured out that people who have frequent ear, nose, throat, and sinus infections are more likely to get meningitis. That is because the same kinds of bacteria that can cause infections in those places are also known to cause meningitis. Since those areas are located close to the brain, bacteria can work their way to the meninges. People are more likely to be at risk for meningitis if they have diabetes or if they have recently had pneumonia, a heart infection, or a head injury.

Poor personal habits can increase a person's chance of getting meningitis. Because alcohol damages cells, excessive drinking can weaken the immune system so that it cannot fight off the viruses or bacteria that cause meningitis. Smoking harms the airways and lessens the ability of immune cells there

Babies naturally get immunities from their mothers, but these usually wear off in a year. Vaccinations, such as those for meningitis, can protect babies after the first year.

to destroy bacteria. That makes it more likely that they could move deeper inside the body and cause illness.

Some factors and healthy personal habits can protect someone from getting meningitis. A person who has had the illness once is less likely to get sick again. This protection is

Scientists must continue the search for new ways to kill the bacteria that cause meningitis. Some forms have become resistant to existing antibiotics.

due to the body's immune response to infectious viruses or bacteria. When the same viruses and bacteria try to invade again, the immune system fights them off with **white blood cells** (WBCs) and **antibodies.** WBCs that have already fought off the infection remain in the bloodstream and in different areas of the body. They are ready to quickly destroy the same kinds of bacteria or viruses again.

Some new mothers who have an immunity, or protection, from meningitis pass it on to their infants. Usually these antibodies disappear in a few months, but by this time the infant has had more time to develop its own immune system.

Today, doctors and researchers continue to look for new ways to fight meningitis. Some researchers are working on new drugs to prevent inflammation in the brain. Other researchers are trying to figure out how to strengthen people's immune systems so they can fight off the viruses and bacteria that cause meningitis. Scientists continue to research more effective vaccines to prevent the infection, as well as antibiotics to cure it before it harms its victims.

3

THE HISTORY OF MENINGITIS

Stories of illnesses that were probably bacterial meningitis date back as long ago as the Middle Ages, from approximately 1300 to 1500. The first medical account of meningitis as a distinct illness seems to be that of Swiss physician Gaspard Vieusseux in 1806, when an epidemic hit Geneva, Switzerland:

At the end of January, in a family composed of a woman and three children, two of the children were attacked and died in less than forty-eight hours. Fifteen days later, the disease appeared in another family in the neighbourhood composed of a father, mother and five infants, four of whom were attacked almost at the same time, and all died from the tenth to the twelfth of February, after having been sick fourteen to fifteen hours with striking symptoms. . . .

Meningitis was called cerebrospinal fever, or brain fever, during the 1800s. No one knew what caused it, but it was

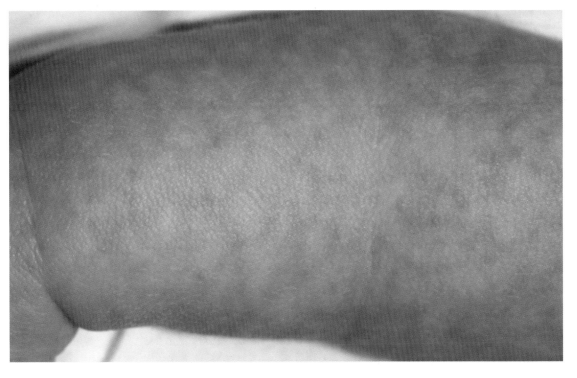

The rash seen in bacterial meningitis meant a death sentence for nearly all victims until antibiotics came into use in the twentieth century.

terrifying and killed far more people than it does today. In the United States, the first recorded epidemic of meningitis was in Massachusetts in 1806. It was called spotted fever at the time, because of a skin rash associated with the infection. (In the United States today, spotted fever refers to a different illness, Rocky Mountain spotted fever, which is a tick-borne disease.)

Not until the 1880s, and the improvement of microscopes, did doctors begin to see that bacteria caused epidemic meningitis. That was around the same time that doctors began to use needles to remove cerebrospinal fluid from the lower

Improved microscopes like this one from the late 1800s made it possible for researchers to see the bacteria that caused meningitis.

back of someone who died of meningitis. The researchers detected bacteria in the fluid. Soon after, in 1887, Austrian scientist Anton Weichselbaum became the first person to identify the same type of bacteria (the meningococcal type) in the spinal fluid of six people who were sick during a meningitis epidemic.

In 1892, a German physician, Richard Friedrich Johannes Pfeiffer, first described another kind of bacteria that causes meningitis, *Haemophilus influenzae*. He came across it in the saliva of people who were sick with influenza, but not meningitis. (That is why the bacteria were given the name *influenzae*.) Years later, however, scientists realized that viruses were the real cause of influenza, and that the *Haemophilus influenzae* bacteria found in people with influenza was causing an additional infection.

Even less than a hundred years ago, nearly every person who caught bacterial meningitis died of it. A historical record of children hospitalized at Boston Children's Hospital in the 1920s shows that only one child survived the illness out of 78 children who had *Haemophilus influenzae* meningitis. Every single one of the 300 children with meningitis caused by pneumococcus-type bacteria died at the hospital. Not quite as many died of meningo-coccus-type bacteria in those days, but it still killed 8 out of 10 people who caught the infection. Those who survived were usually blind or deaf for the rest of their lives.

Today, the death rate from meningitis remains high in

The Meningitis Belt

Meningitis occurs all over the world, but there are places where epidemics happen more often than elsewhere. In Africa there is an area called the "meningitis belt," which includes several countries just south of the Sahara Desert. Meningitis epidemics are common there. In 1996, for example, over 250,000 people became ill in that area, and approximately 25,000 of them died.

Because there is little rainfall between December and June in these parts of the world, people inhale dust, which may carry meningitis bacteria and irritate windpipes and lungs. Also, many people are poor and live in crowded conditions. They lack clean water, nutritious food, and good health care. All of those things make it more likely that they will get sick and spread the illness around.

countries where people have not been vaccinated or received effective medications. That is the case in several sub-Saharan African countries. For those people living in countries with good medical services, the situation has reversed. Most people do recover from meningitis without long-term problems.

EARLY TREATMENTS

In the 1800s, treatments for meningitis were very different from today. Doctors cared for patients by giving them substances that would clean out the stomach and intestines. One of the substances was mercury, which is now known to be highly toxic, or poisonous. Sweating also was thought to be helpful. Doctors placed pieces of boiled hemlock wood beside the patient to make them sweat. Some physicians recommended that their patients drink wine in the belief that it would be helpful in ridding the body of the infection. Toward the end of the 1800s, doctors commonly removed some of the patient's cerebrospinal fluid by spinal tap over and over in an attempt to drain the infection from the body. Unfortunately, these treatments did not work. In those days, someone who got bacterial meningitis was much more likely to die than to survive.

A type of antibiotic called **sulfonamides** was the first effective medication doctors used to help kill meningitis bacteria. The use of sulfonamides in the 1930s brought down the death rate. In the past, most victims died from bacterial meningitis, but the death rate in the United States now ranges between 5 and 15 percent. Sulfonamides are not used much today, although doctors will sometimes prescribe them for people who are allergic to antibiotics or if antibiotics do not work on them.

Doctors also found they could save lives by giving patients **antiserum** made from the blood of living animals, usually rabbits. The animals were deliberately infected with meningitis bacteria. This caused their immune systems to produce effective antibodies that could destroy the bacteria. The animal blood was then injected into the person infected with meningitis in the hope that the animal's antibodies would kill off the bacteria. While the treatment did work at times, it also caused many serious allergic reactions. Fortunately, the discovery of antibiotics replaced antiserums. And best of all, vaccinations greatly lessened the occurrence of several types of meningitis so that people did not get meningitis as often.

Antibiotics

Antibiotics are medications that kill bacteria or make them unable to spread further. The Scottish scientist Alexander Fleming discovered the first antibiotic, called **penicillin,** in 1928. After Fleming's discovery, two other scientists figured out how to make penicillin into a medication that would kill

Alexander Fleming's discovery of penicillin greatly reduced death rates of people with bacterial meningitis.

infectious bacteria, including meningitis. Those men, Howard Florey and Ernst Boris Chain, won the Nobel Prize in 1945, along with Alexander Fleming, for their work.

Penicillin and some very similar antibiotics are still used to treat bacterial meningitis today. Because bacteria can change or mutate over time, old antibiotics are no longer effective against them. Researchers and doctors continue to develop newer antibiotics, just to keep up with the changing bacteria.

Those of us who live in areas where medical care is good may not realize that in some parts of the world, these life-saving antibiotics are hard to get. They can be too expensive

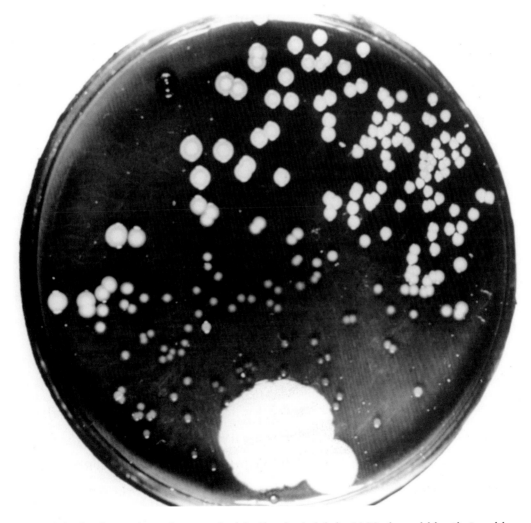

This original culture plate photographed in Fleming's lab in 1928 showed him that mold had properties that could kill bacteria.

for some people, and doctors and hospitals are too far away for people who live out in the countryside. Fortunately, organizations around the world are looking for ways to get antibiotics to these people more easily and inexpensively.

Vaccinations

The number of people who die today from bacterial meningitis has been greatly reduced, thanks to vaccines that prevent the infection in the first place. The children and adults who get vaccinations actually get shots of weakened bacteria of the type that cause the deadly infection. But these amounts are usually harmless to nearly everyone who gets the shot. The presence of the bacteria triggers a person's immune system to make antibodies that recognize the bacteria and kill them. Later, if the same type of meningitis bacteria tries to attack, immune system cells "remember" them and produce the same antibodies again.

Today, doctors and researchers continue to develop new vaccines in addition to the Hib vaccine now recommended for all babies. Researchers are involved in promising research into the next-most-needed vaccine, one for the Group B form of meningitis. Although many antibiotics and vaccinations work well now, researchers are working on new ones that will make meningitis an infection of the past.

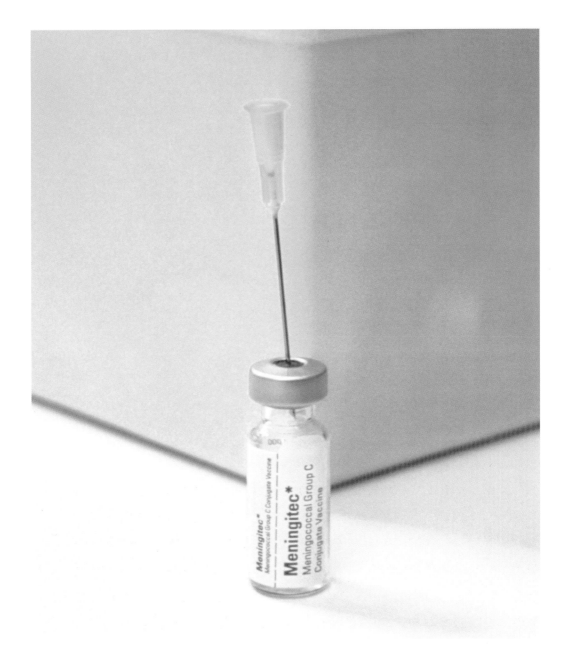

Death rates have been cut in countries where vaccination rates are high. More work needs to be done to get effective vaccines to countries where vaccination rates are still low.

4

DIAGNOSING, TREATING, AND COPING WITH MENINGITIS

I magine you are a doctor, trying to figure out if someone has meningitis. What symptoms do you look for? First, the doctor collects a lot of information about the person. This information provides the clues the doctor will use to make a **diagnosis,** which is the doctor's decision about what is wrong. The first diagnosis is not always correct, and the diagnosis must be changed as more clues are discovered.

One kind of information a doctor collects is the patient's "history." This means anything about past illnesses or health problems. For example, if a patient has had another illness recently, this can help a doctor decide whether an infection might still be present somewhere. A person who recently has had a throat or ear infection is more likely to have meningitis than a person who has been healthy.

The next way a doctor collects information is by performing a physical exam. During the exam, the doctor looks for other

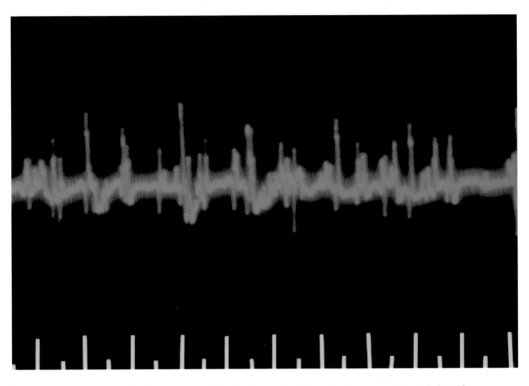

Doctors may use an electromyogram to test a patient's nerve or muscle activity if meningitis is suspected.

clues about what might be making the patient ill. A **neurological examination** tests how well the brain is controlling the body's many activities. The doctor will have the person do simple things such as bending, walking, and balancing to examine how well muscles and reflexes are working. Doctors also test a patient's hearing, speaking, and vision. The neurological examination will also include questions to see whether the person is thinking clearly or not. Confusion and memory loss can be signs of brain injury.

Laboratory tests of blood, urine, and cerebrospinal fluid provide more clues. Urine and blood samples can indicate whether there are bacteria circulating through the patient's body.

Getting a sample of cerebrospinal fluid is a little harder, but it is necessary if the doctor suspects meningitis. To sample the CSF, a spinal tap, or lumbar puncture (lumbar refers to the lower back area), is done. First, the person is given a shot of anesthetic around the lower part of the spine to numb that area. Then a needle is pushed in gently until it barely pierces the meninges. A small amount of fluid is removed. If meningitis is strongly suspected, doctors do this as soon as possible so that they can administer antibiotics right after the spinal tap.

Doctors and lab technicians look for signs of infection by

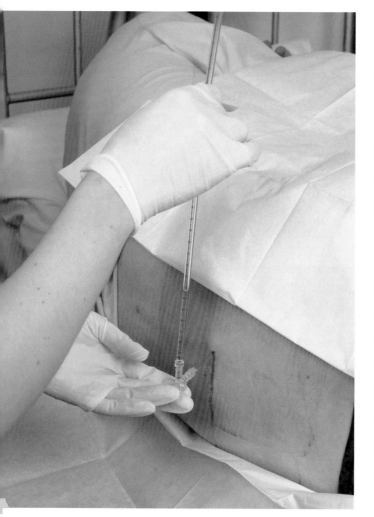

A doctor is collecting cerebrospinal fluid from a patient during a spinal tap. The large brownish area on the patient's back comes from a liquid used to keep germs away from the puncture area.

studying CSF samples. They may look under a microscope for the actual organism that might be causing the infection. They will check the quantities of white blood cells (WBCs) in these fluids, too. The number of WBCs goes up when the body is fighting an infection. A very strong clue that a person has meningitis is the presence of WBCs in the cerebrospinal fluid, which usually has none.

Doctors might also do a **throat culture** to see whether bacteria that can cause meningitis are living in the person's throat. A technician collects a sample of saliva and mucus from the back of the patient's throat with a cotton swab. In the laboratory, the swab is rinsed with a special liquid that will keep cells and bacteria alive. That liquid is kept for several days to see if any meningitis-causing bacteria are growing in it. This takes days because bacteria are so small, that they need time to multiply so that there are enough to be studied.

Another way to see whether a person might have meningitis is to take computer images of the brain and spinal cord areas. For example, one type of machine sends X rays (a type of invisible energy beam) into the person's body and records how well those X rays pass through. Then the computer creates a picture, which may show swollen meninges. The picture is called a **CT scan** or CAT scan (CT stands for computerized tomography; CAT for computerized axial tomography). CT scans show much more detailed images than ordinary X rays do alone. A second kind of

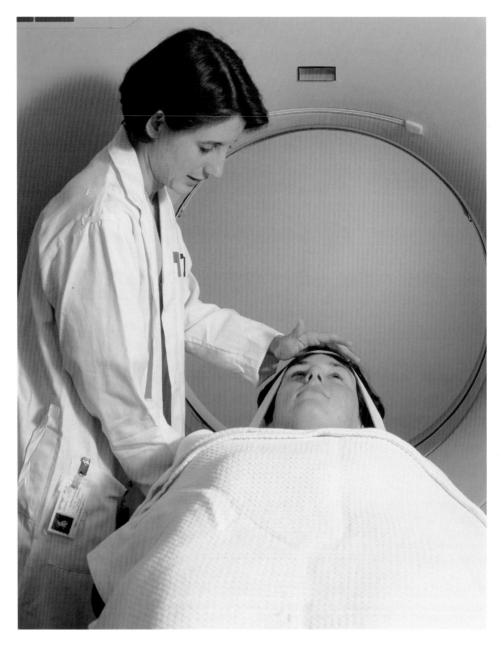

A CT scan gives doctors a way of looking inside the brain and spine for infection or damage.

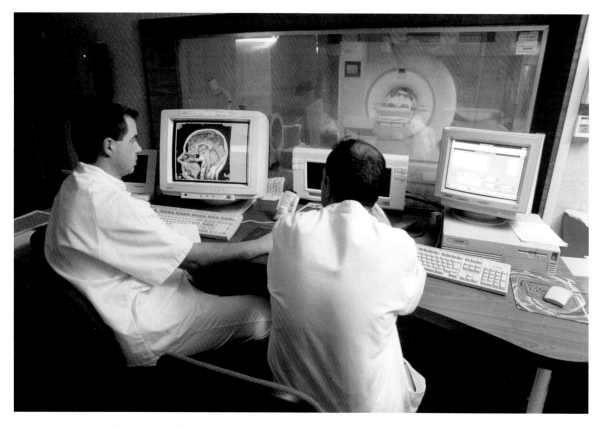

These radiologists are doctors who use MRI scans to make diagnoses of infections such as meningitis. The MRI machine uses powerful magnets and radio waves to show slices of the brain or other body parts.

imaging machine is called an **MRI** (magnetic resonance imaging). MRIs use a different kind of energy beam (radio waves) to collect information about the inside of the body. The computer then takes the information to make an even more detailed picture. Undergoing a CT scan or MRI is painless. All the patient needs to do is lie very still so that the machines can get accurate information.

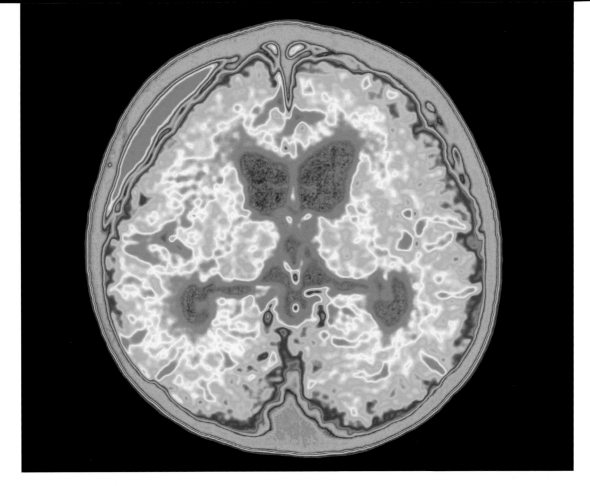

This MRI brain scan of a seven-month-old baby displays a meningitis infection in the upper left of the picture (shown in red).

One more test a doctor may order is an **EEG** (short for electroencephalogram). This is a simple, painless way of measuring the brain's electrical activity. Infections in or around the brain can cause unusual electrical activity, which the doctor will notice.

The doctor pulls together information from all of these tests to make a diagnosis and recommend the best treatment. If there is a possibility of meningitis, treatment will begin immediately. Doctors may begin antibiotic treatment before some test results come in. When it comes to bacterial meningitis, getting medication started is more urgent than getting a definite diagnosis.

TREATMENTS

If a doctor suspects that a person has bacterial meningitis, the patient may be isolated in a private room to protect others from being exposed to the infection. Usually, the medical staff begins giving the patient massive amounts of antibiotics

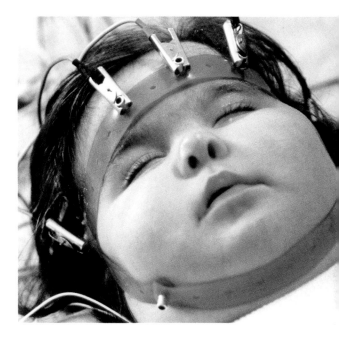

The EEG electrodes on this sleeping toddler's scalp test for possible abnormal brain activity that an infection may have caused.

through an IV to destroy them. Penicillin or similar antibiotics are used, sometimes combined with newer antibiotics to ensure that as many types of bacteria are killed as possible.

Although antibiotics do not get rid of viruses in viral meningitis, it is better to get a person started on antibiotics even before doctors know whether the patient has the bacterial or viral form of meningitis. People with viral meningitis can stop taking the antibiotics during their recovery, which will take place over several days or a few weeks. During that time, the immune system usually takes care of the viral infection. If a fungus has caused the meningitis, doctors will prescribe antifungal medications that will help destroy the fungus. Doctors might also give medications that reduce swelling in the meninges. Doing so may prevent hearing loss.

Some doctors use drugs to put a very sick patient into a coma. Because an infection such as bacterial meningitis can cause so much swelling, brain damage is a danger. A medical coma slows down swelling that might cause permanent injury to the brain and spinal column.

Medications can also be given to lessen headache pain and lower fever. Additionally, someone with complications may need to be hospitalized to receive fluids and nutrition if he or she cannot eat solid food.

RECOVERY

Nearly everyone who gets viral meningitis will recover within a week or two with simple treatment of symptoms at home. And most people with the more serious form, bacterial meningitis, who get immediate and thorough medical care, recover fully within a few weeks. Some people, however, have lasting problems because meningitis can damage brain cells as well as other organ cells. Several of the problems may go away, while some are permanent. They include having seizures, poor muscle control, learning difficulties, poor eyesight or blindness, and hearing loss, including total deafness. Bacteria also can damage the kidneys, the organs that cleanse the blood and make urine, and the adrenal glands, which produce various hormones and control many body functions. Those problems can become very serious. When blood poisoning appears with meningitis, bacteria may destroy too many blood vessels. Surgery may be needed to remove damaged tissues in arms, fingers, legs, feet, and toes.

Doctors have noticed other changes in their patients as they recover from meningitis. Some patients have strong mood swings, temper tantrums, or surprising anger and violence. It is not clear whether or not these changes are due to brain damage or the long, difficult recovery.

Fortunately, there are specially trained people to help

Meningitis survivors who have lost limbs to the infection may walk again and even play sports with the help of artificial limbs.

victims of meningitis learn how to cope with physical changes. A speech therapist or hearing specialist can help a person deal with hearing loss. A social worker or psychologist can help a

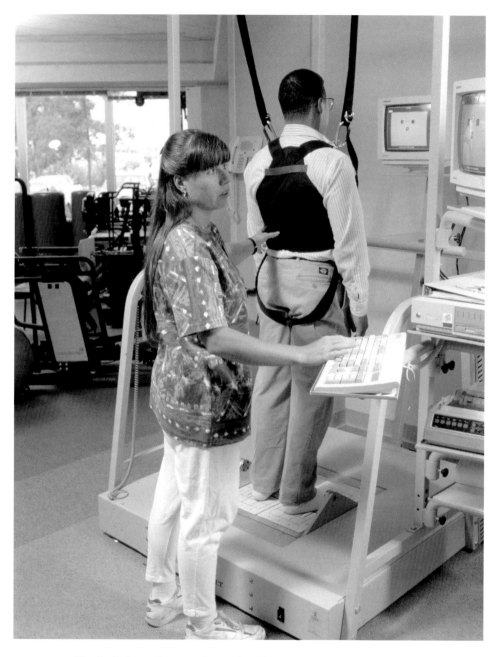

Physical therapists teach meningitis patients to walk again.

meningitis survivor express feelings and recover emotionally from the illness. Hospitals and special organizations invite people who have had meningitis, and their families, to gather together and share their stories about how they got through the hard times, and how they are making a comeback to an enriching, happy life.

PREVENTING MENINGITIS

Vaccination is one of the most effective ways to stop people from getting meningitis in the first place. Childhood vaccinations can prevent many cases of meningitis. The first vaccine to prevent meningitis was the Hib vaccine, which is now given to all children in countries with a high level of medical care. This has greatly decreased the number of Hib meningitis cases. There are two vaccines for pneumococcal meningitis. Doctors give one kind to adults at high risk for infection and one to all children in countries with well-developed vaccination programs. The newest vaccine covers meningococcal meningitis. Doctors recommend giving this vaccine to eleven and twelve year olds. Those who do not receive it as preteens should get the vaccine before they enter college or the military. This is because they will be living in close quarters with other young, possibly at-risk people.

Good **hygiene** (cleanliness) is another important part of preventing meningitis. Cleanliness can stop the spread of bacteria and viruses among people. That means washing hands

Meningitis patients who have lost their hearing may learn to speak again through sign language.

before eating, after using the bathroom, and after being around people who are sneezing and coughing.

A healthy immune system can often fight off the infection. Eating nutritious foods such as fruits and vegetables can provide the nutrition that immune system cells need to do their jobs effectively.

Since people who live closely together or spend a lot of time together are more likely to spread meningitis around, it is a good idea to notice any symptoms that you, your friends, or family members might have. Anyone who has symptoms such as a severe, worsening headache, a very painful neck, a fever, mental confusion, sore legs, or a rash should be checked out by a doctor immediately. Early treatment can save lives.

Meningitis vaccinations during childhood, adolescence, and early adulthood have greatly cut the rate of infection in young people.

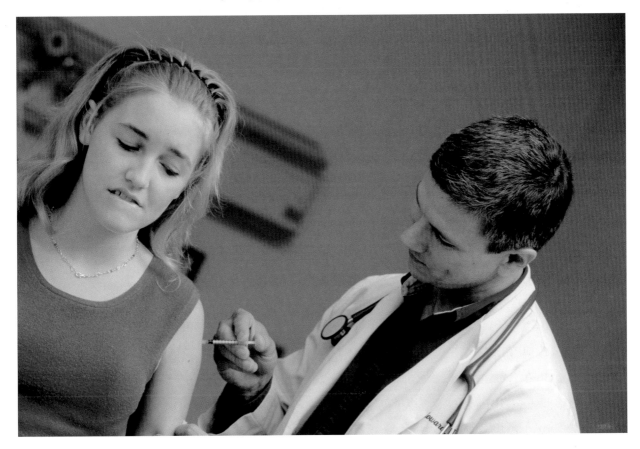

GLOSSARY

amputation—The surgery to remove damaged body tissues in arms, legs, fingers, or toes.

antibiotics—The medications that either kill bacteria or stop them from spreading.

antibodies—The small protein particles that help fight infection by sticking to bacteria and making them easier for the immune system to identify and destroy.

antiserum—A part of animal blood used to treat some diseases.

bacteria—The one-celled microorganisms that sometimes cause infection.

bacterial meningitis—The kind of meningitis that bacteria cause.

blood pressure—The pressure created in blood vessels by the pumping of the heart, which keeps blood moving.

cells—The smallest living units that make up people, animals, plants, and other life forms.

cerebrospinal—Referring to the brain and spinal cord together. Cerebrospinal fluid is a liquid that keeps the brain and spinal cord moist and healthy.

coma—A state of unconsciousness caused by serious injury or illness.

CT scan (or CAT scan)—A picture of the inside of the body, made by sending X rays through the body and using computers to make the final picture.

diagnosis—A doctor's decision about what illness a person has.

EEG—(electroencephalogram) A painless measure of the brain's electrical activity, which helps a doctor to see whether there is an infection or other problem in the brain.

electromyogram—a machine that measure electrical activity in muscles.

encephalitis—An infection in the brain, which causes inflammation.

epidemics—Situations in which many people have the same kind of illness at the same time and are probably spreading it to other people.

epiglottitis—An infection of the tissues at the back of the tongue.

feces—The waste matter left over and excreted after food is digested.

gangrene—The death of body tissue due to poor blood supply.

hygiene—The practices that help prevent illnesses, mainly through cleanliness.

immune system—The body's team of special cells and antibodies that work together to destroy viruses, bacteria, and other things that can cause illness.

infection—An injury that harmful bacteria, viruses, parasites, or other organisms cause when they enter the body.

inflammation—The body's response to injury, which helps heal the injured area, but which can also harm the body by causing too much swelling and pressure.

intravenous (IV)—Given by way of a needle inserted into a blood vessel.

meninges—The three-layered covering that protects the brain and spinal cord.

meningoccal meningitis—The form of meningitis caused by the bacteria *Neisseria meningitis,* which are responsible for epidemics.

MRI (magnetic resonance imaging)— A technique that takes detailed pictures of the inside of the body.

mucus—The slimy substance produced in the nose and windpipe to protect against harmful germs and viruses.

mutate—To cause a change in cell structure.

myelitis—An infection in the spinal cord.

neurological examination—One of a doctor's ways to tell how well the brain is working.

neurons—The types of cells found in the brain, spinal cord, and throughout the body.

penicillin—An important antibiotic medication used to treat meningitis.

pneumoccocal meningitis—The form of meningitis caused by *Streptococcus pneumoniae* bacteria, which also may cause ear infections.

septicemia—A bacterial infection of the blood or blood poisoning.

seizures—The sudden unplanned tightening of muscles caused by infection or brain injury.

spinal cord—A bundle of neurons running inside the vertebral column (spine), from the brain down to the tailbone. It carries messages among neurons throughout the body and the brain.

spinal tap (lumbar puncture)—A procedure that samples the cerebrospinal fluid around the spinal cord using a needle.

spleen—An organ that is part of the immune system.

sulfonamides—One of a class of drugs first used to kill bacteria.

throat culture—A sample taken from someone's throat and tested in a laboratory for signs of bacteria.

toxins—The poisons that some microorganisms, such as bacteria, produce.

vaccination—The injection of a substance that protects a healthy person from foreign invaders such as bacteria and viruses.

vertebral column—The group of disk-shaped bones, stacked on one another, that run down the back and protect the enclosed spinal cord. It is also called the spine.

viral meningitis—The kind of meningitis that viruses cause.

viruses—The particles that must infect another organism in order to reproduce.

WBCs (white blood cells)—Cells that are part of the immune system, protecting the body against infections.

FIND OUT MORE

Organizations

Center for Disease Control and Prevention
1600 Clifton Road
Atlanta, Georgia 30333
Phone: 1-800-311-3435
Web site: http://www.cdc.gov

Meningitis Foundation of America
6610 North Shadeland Station, Suite 220
Indianapolis, IN 46220-4393
Phone: 1-800-668-1129
Web site: http://www.musa.org

National Meningitis Association
738 Robinson Farms Drive
Marietta, GA 30068
Phone: 1-866-FONE-NMA
Web site: http://www.nmaus.org

Books

Routh, Kristina. *Meningitis*. Chicago, IL: Heinemann, 2004.

Shmaefsky, Brian, and Alcamo, I. Edward. *Meningitis*. New York: Chelsea House Publications, 2004.

Willett, Edward. *Meningitis*. Berkeley Heights, NJ: Enslow Publishers, 1999.

Web Sites

KidsHealth for Kids—Meningitis
http://www.kidshealth.org/kid/health_problems/brain/meningitis.html

Meningitis Research Foundation
http://www.meningitis.org

National Foundation for Infectious Diseases
http://www.nfid.org/content/meningitis

INDEX

ABOUT THE AUTHOR

Lorrie Klosterman writes and teaches about animal biology and human health for all ages. She is constantly amazed by the way all of the world's organisms interact.